BONFIRE

The Lewes Bonfire Societies in photographs

Jim Etherington

S.B. Publications

By the same author:
Lewes Bonfire Night: A short history of the Guy Fawkes celebrations.

First published by S.B. Publications
19 Grove Road, Seaford, East Sussex BN25 1TP

ISBN 1 85770 142 9

Front cover: Commercial Square passing under the Castle Barbican.
(Photo: Tizzie Knowles)

Back cover: Commercial Square processing down School Hill.
(Photo: Peter Schueler)

Title page: Cliffe members await the start of the barrel race.
(Photo: Sussex Express)

Typeset and Printed by Island Press
3 Cradle Hill Industrial Estate, Seaford, East Sussex BN25 3JE   Tel: 01323 490222

Acknowledgements

Sincere thanks are due to Tizzie Knowles for undertaking the role of second photographer and to Peter Schueler and Sussex Express for making available additional photographs. Without their help the coverage achieved on the 'Fifth' would not have been as comprehensive.

I am also indebted to the Lewes Bonfire Societies for their co-operation, in particular Cliffe, Commercial Square and Waterloo, whose members patiently tolerated the presence of photographers and whose willing assistance made this book possible.

Photographs

Jim Etherington 2-42, 47, 57-8, 62, 68, 74, 77-80, 92-3, 95-6, 98-100, 103-4, 106-09

Tizzie Knowles 43-6, 48-56, 63-7, 69, 71, 75, 90, 97, 101-2, 105

Peter Schueler 1, 60, 77, 81, 86-9, 94

Sussex Express 59, 61, 70, 72-3, 76, 82-5, 91

1. Lewes Bonfire Night - a spectacle to be watched.

Introduction

For the thousands of spectators who throng the streets of Lewes every 5th November to witness the annual Guy Fawkes Night celebrations the spectacular processions and firework displays they witness represent just one night of the year. But 'Bonfire Night', as it is known locally, is the climax of a year's work for the members of the five Lewes Bonfire Societies. The following photographs chronicle their members' activities as they prepare for and carry out the 1996 Guy Fawkes Night celebrations.

The bonfire societies rely on their own resources to raise the necessary funds to hire bands, purchase torch making materials and buy fireworks for their celebrations. Under the leadership of committees each undertake fundraising throughout the year including jumble sales, recycling waste paper, fêtes and fairs. Fundraising has a social dimension and the societies promote this further by arranging events for their members like picnics, treasure hunts, excursions to the races and sporting fixtures against local teams. Members are also active at home making the costumes they will wear on the 'Fifth'.

During early September preparations for the 'Fifth' commence. Led by 'Captains', groups of bonfire boys and girls begin their appointed tasks. Experienced pyrotechnists start constructing the tableau that will be the centre piece of the firesite firework display. Traditional effigies of Guy Fawkes and Pope Paul V are made and set pieces used during the processions prepared. Torchmakers gather Sunday mornings to make the thousands of torches required to illuminate the numerous processions that will perambulate the town during the celebrations.

Through October societies hold their own fancy dress competitions culminating in the Lewes Bonfire Council's Fancy Dress Competition at the Town hall. The inter-society rivalry here is intense, each striving to be the best dressed society in Lewes. Saturday mornings see costumed members in the High Street selling programmes while others start building bonfires at the various firesites. This is also the 'out-meeting' season when coaches taking members to similar celebrations in neighbouring towns and villages leave Lewes each Saturday evening.

In the final days leading up to the 'Fifth' various gatherings occur. On the Sunday prior to the 'Fifth' the Annual Thanksgiving Service is held at Jireh Chapel. On 3rd November marshals gather to receive instructions from the Commander-in-chief to ensure the smooth running of the processions. The next night each society holds Badge Night at its headquarters when members pay their 'subs' and collect badges to be worn the following evening.

Before sunrise on the appointed day final preparations are undertaken. Torches are dipped in paraffin and distributed around the town, tableaux and effigies taken to secret locations in readiness and at firesites scaffold frames for setpieces and clergy platforms erected. By mid-day local hostelries are the venue for excited conversation and refreshment.

Lewes starts to burn at 5.30pm and continues until the last embers are extinguished just after midnight. Some societies open their proceedings with childrens' processions, others with lively barrel races. All recite 'Bonfire Prayers', the traditional 'Remember, remember' rhyme. The early part of the evening sees the five societies, Cliffe, Commercial Square, Lewes Borough, South Street and Waterloo parading through different areas of the town, each visiting Cliffe Bridge, to throw a blazing barrel into the River Ouse, and the War Memorial where wreaths are laid by the Presidents of each society and appropriate firework displays ignited. Towards 7.30 the societies, except Cliffe (and exceptionally South Street in 1997), converge on St Anne's Crescent to form the Grand United Procession. This impressive procession proceeds down the High Street before dispersing at Library Corner, each society returning to its headquarters in readiness for its own 'Grand' procession to the firesite.

Between 9.00 and 10.30 visitors have the choice of five firesites where they gather in large numbers to be addressed by the society's 'Archbishop', warmed by the bonfire and impressed by a firework display of tableau, effigies and aerial rockets. The evening closes with each society's last procession arriving at traditional locations for the building of small fires, the singing of 'Auld Lang Syne' and a final rendition of 'Bonfire Prayers'.

The 'Bonfire' year is not quite over. Final gatherings bring society members together to recount another successful 'Fifth' and prepare for the next. The proceeds of the charity collections are counted on Box Night, the evening after the 'Fifth'. During December annual dinners are held, before finally at annual general meetings officers and committees are elected, charged with the responsibility of organising next year's Lewes Guy Fawkes Night celebrations.

2/3. Cliffe (top) and Commercial Square (bottom) committee members.

4. Bundling newspapers for recycling to raise funds.

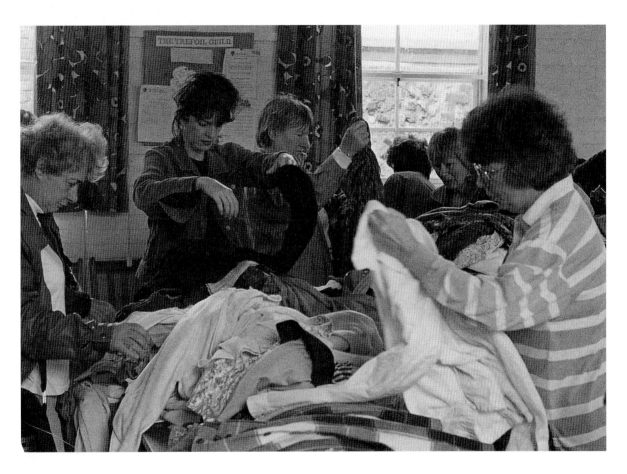

5. Jumble sales - the traditional fundraiser.

6. A day at the races - Cliffe at Glorious Goodwood.

7. Cliffe Bonfire Society 'R.F.C.'.

8. Cliffe applauded from the pitch by the Elephant and Castle rugby team.

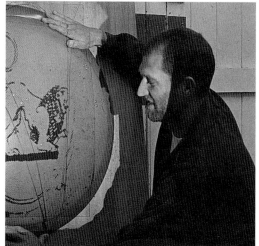

9/11. Greek Hoplite, second pioneer costume of Waterloo, in the early stages of making.

12. Borough member putting the finishing touches to his zulu head-dress.

13/14. Chicken wire and papier mâché - Waterloo's 'tab' in the making.

15/16. Teabreak and a return to work for the
Cliffe 'tab' builders.

17. The B.S.E. threat emerges - the near completed Cliffe tableau.

18. Cliffe effigy maker.

19. Poppies being cleaned in readiness for the Cliffe's War Memorial ceremony.

20. Dusting down Waterloo's 'Guy Fawkes' after a year in store.

21. The Commercial Square Bonfire Society torchmakers.

22. Making torches at Waterloo.

23/24. Commercial Square fancy
dress competition winner.

25. Young sundancer with proud dad at Commercial.

26. Judge and competitor chat at Waterloo's fancy dress competition.

27. Winning the cup as Waterloo's best dressed lady.

28. Signing the certificates.

29. Waiting to enter the Town
    Hall at the Bonfire Council's
    fancy dress competition.

26

30. A Borough zulu waits in the Corn Exchange.

31. Waterloo's Greek hoplites in the second pioneer class.

32. Tudor children from Waterloo.

33. Commercial members leave for an 'out meeting'.

34. Waterloo family visit Littlehampton.

35. Building the bonfire at Cliffe.

36. Waterloo's chairman's window display.

37. Annual Thanksgiving Service, Jireh Chapel.

38. Commercial Square programme sellers.

39/40. Marshals receiving final instructions from the
Commander-in-Chief at Cliffe.

41. Badge Night at the Elephant and Castle, headquarters of the Commercial Square.

42. Sunrise on the 'Fifth' - Cliffe 'tab' ready to be moved.

43. Borough's torchdipping ramp.

44. The 'No Popery' banner across Cliffe High Street.

45. 'Guy Fawkes intent to blow up the King and the Parliament'.

46. Commercial remember Dunblane at its Landport firesite.

47. The Commercial Square 'foremen'.

48. The clergy platform erected on
    Commercial's firesite.

49. Preparations at Waterloo's firesite.

50. Borough's key, letters and cross ready to be carried in the evening's processions.

51. Borough's barrel carts ready to be taken into Lewes.

52. Lunch time at Commercial Square.

53. Refreshments before policing the 'Fifth'.

54. Set up to feed hundreds of hungry spectators.

55. Windows protected.

Society badges head the processions.

56. Waterloo Bonfire Society.

57. South Street Bonfire Society.

58. Cliffe Bonfire Society.

59. Borough Bonfire Society.

60. The indian head badge of Commercial Square Bonfire Society.

61. Ladies of the Cliffe race the barrels.

62. A more sedate pace for the trolley loaded with tar barrels.

63. Early evening 'Bonfire Prayers' start Commercial's proceedings.

Young members with their parents.

64. Borough 'smugglers'.

65. Commercial indians.

66. The Borough's President selling programmes.

67. Raising money for charity - Commercial Square's Captain of Boxes.

68. Youth band accompanying a procession.

69. The Corps of the Royal Engineers provide music for Waterloo.

70. A veteran member of South Street.

71. Borough zulu 'pioneer'.

72. The Cliffe's naval contingent.

73. Borough's barrel - destination, the River Ouse.

74. South Street moving towards the War Memorial.

75. Commercial's President waiting to lay the wreath at the War Memorial.

76. Borough's War Memorial guard of honour.

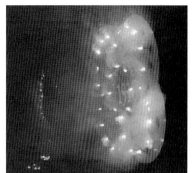

Poignant reminders.

77. Cliffe's poppies burn.

78. Cliffe's set piece waits to be ignited.

79. Cliffe moves away from the War Memorial.

80. Cliffe remembers the Lewes Protestant Martyrs.

81. Waiting to form up for the United Grand Procession.

82. The Lewes Bonfire Council banner leads the 'United Grand'.

83. Bonfire Boys fall out - South Street tableau.

84. Borough's response to considered unnecessary intervention.

85. The brighter side of policing.

86. Commercial Square's barrels pass through the 'bottle neck'.

87. Borough's motto and 'burning letters'.

88. Commercial Square 'pioneers' lead their 'Grand Procession' through the High Street.

89. The North American theme continued in Commercial's setpiece display.

90. Guy Fawkes in Waterloo's procession.

91. Ghengiz Khan tableau rides with Waterloo.

92. Viking and priest enjoy a joke waiting for the procession to move off.

93. Cliffe turning into Friars Walk from School Hill.

94. Commercial Apaches.

95. Cliffe Voluntary Fire Brigade - a replica of the past.

96. Pope Paul V borne aloft to Cliffe's firesite.

97. Clergy platform - Commercial Square firesite.

98. Costumed spectators - Cliffe members look on.

Cliffe's Archbishop and Clergy

99. Waiting to mount the platform.

100. Addressing the crowd.

101. Firework shell burst over South Street.

102. Mortars erupt at Commercial Square.

103. Cliffe's tableau begins to explode.

104. Waterloo's closing street fire.

105. Midnight - Bonfire Prayers in Commercial Square.

106. Counting the money at Cliffe's Box Night.

107. Waterloo's Annual Dinner - the Chairman's speech.

Commercial Square's Annual General Meeting.

108. Members consider issues.

109. Officers await decisions.